Y0-AQL-664

WRESTLING WITH OBEDIENCE

WRESTLING WITH

Obedience

JOY P. GAGE

VICTOR BOOKS®

A DIVISION OF SCRIPTURE PRESS PUBLICATIONS INC.
USA CANADA ENGLAND

Portions of this material appeared previously in *Lord, Can We Talk This Over?* (Moody Press, 1977).

Scripture quotations are from the *Holy Bible, New International Version*, © 1973, 1978, 1984, International Bible Society. Used by permission of Zondervan Bible Publishers.

Recommended Dewey Decimal Classification: 222.12
Suggested Subject Heading: BIBLE, O.T.: EXODUS

Library of Congress Catalog Card Number: 90-24447
ISBN: 0-89693-147-1

1 2 3 4 5 6 7 8 9 10 Printing/Year 95 94 93 92 91

© 1991 by SP Publications, Inc. All rights reserved. Printed in the United States of America. No part of this book may be reproduced without written permission, except for brief quotations in books, critical articles, and reviews.

VICTOR BOOKS
A division of SP Publications, Inc.
Wheaton, Illinois 60187

CONTENTS

Wrestling with God! The very phrase brings to mind one Old Testament character—Jacob. Jacob did indeed wrestle with that Divine Presence, but he wasn't the only one. In the Scriptures we find many examples of people who have wrestled with God.

Hebrews 11, known as "Faith's Hall of Fame," includes a number of people who resisted God's claims on their lives. After much wrestling with Him, they went on to become "heroes of faith." In this passage, where faith and obedience are used almost interchangeably, numerous individuals are said to have exercised faith through obedience. Yet an examination of their earlier lives will reveal that they often struggled with God over the very issue of obedience.

"I'm not the man for this job," one said in an attempt to enlighten God.

"I have a better plan," one informed Him.

"It's been tried before," one reminded Him.

"It'll never work," one argued with Him.

Moses used all these excuses and more. Yet there came a time when he became a model of obedience. His exemplary obedience is examined in my book, *A Heart for Obedience* [Victor], a study on the last days of Moses' life as seen in Deuteronomy. In Hebrews 11, Moses commands more space than any other individual except Abraham. But Moses was a man for whom obedience did not come easily.

At the burning bush, he wrestled with God. He didn't want to do what God wanted him to do. He didn't think he could. He didn't want to try. "Just send somebody else," he told God.

When he finally obeyed, he did so reluctantly and then wrestled with God over the lack of results. "Why have You brought me here?" he demanded. His many conversations with God reflect his ongoing struggle over obedience. They also emphasize the fact that no matter how great the struggle, Moses' obedience continued to develop because Moses continued to obey—whether he wanted to or not.

At the burning bush, we hear him say, "Lord, I can't, I can't, I can't."

On the mountaintop of Sinai, we hear him say, "Lord, You promised, You promised, You promised." How did he get from the "burning bush" to the "mountaintop"?

By examining this question, we can discover eight very important principles for our own growth.

Using this Study Guide
The book of Exodus records Israel's exit from Egypt. Because we are approaching it from the viewpoint of one person and what God did in his life, we will not examine every chapter.

Each study begins with *Discovery Time,* a guided study which develops observations, interpretation, and application skills. You will notice a recurring heading in each of the *Discovery Time* sections—"Put yourself in Moses' sandals." This feature is included to encourage personal application.

The *Digest* section is provided as a commentary on the theme for that session. Read it after you have completed the personal study. If you are using this guide for group study, underline anything you do not understand and ask for clarification. Make a note of additional thoughts you may have which will add to the group discussion on this lesson.

The *Personal Response Journal* is for recording impressions from the lesson. Each journal includes a "thought starter" to get you going. But these are only suggestions. Make this section uniquely yours. It is not to be shared with the group.

A *Growth Chart* is provided at the conclusion of chapter eight. This chart is to be referred to each week. It will help you trace the growth of Moses' obedience, step by step. The last *Discovery Time* question in each lesson instructs you to add a specific growth step to the chart. By keeping up with the chart, you will be reminded each week of how obedience grows one step at a time. Like all growth charts, it measures from the bottom up. The first step is filled in to show you how it works. If you like, fill in the chart with simple drawings, mottoes, or stickers to illustrate the steps each week.

Diversify is a resource section for all who may be leading a group through this study. This section offers practical suggestions for enriching the group time. While there are specific instructions for each chapter, feel free to adapt, add, or change them according to the needs of your group.

CHAPTER ONE

❧ DISCOVERY TIME ❧

Read Exodus 1:1–2:15.

1. Jot down general impressions of this period of Israel's history and/or some ways it specifically affected one family.

2. From the following passages, summarize your observations about the political situation in Egypt.

   Exodus 1:6-9

   Exodus 1:10

   Exodus 1:11-14

3. Summarize the population control method devised by Pharaoh (1:15-21).

4. Compare Exodus 2:1-3, Acts 7:19, and Hebrews 11:23. What do these Scriptures tell us about Moses' parents?

5. Review Exodus 1:22–2:10. Assume you are a newspaper journalist and have been given an assignment to do a story on the events covered in this passage.

What headline would you choose?

What would be your lead?

How would you summarize the events?

6. Read Acts 7:17-36 to get an overview of the events of Exodus 1–2 as seen in Stephen's sermon. Describe what Moses' life must have been like as the adopted son of Pharaoh's daughter and how it differed from that of a slave child.

7. Compare Exodus 2:11, Acts 7:23-25, and Hebrews 11:24-25. Based on all these passages, what do you think influenced Moses to visit the brickyards?

8. Review Hebrews 11:24-25. In what ways does this passage speak of commitment?

9. In what way did the events of Exodus 2:11-15 change the course of Moses' life?

10. Summarize the events of Exodus 2:16-22 noting the people, place, and events.

11. What significance do you see in 2:22?

12. The Scriptures give no indication that Moses struggled with his decision to forsake his standing in the palace in order to identify himself with the slaves; however, it is easy to see how any one of us would struggle over a decision of this magnitude. How many things can you think of that Moses had to give up in making his choice?

Put Yourself in Moses' Sandals
13. You are a wealthy, educated woman. In response to an unmistakable call of God, you dispose of your possessions and become part of a group of people (homeless, immigrants, HIV-infected, etc.) in order to help them. Your first very bold attempt to improve their situation ends disastrously and you are forced to leave the job immediately. What would be your reaction or thoughts concerning . . .

the price of your commitment to this cause

the validity of your "clear call" from God

your failure to accomplish what you set out to do

your availability to God for a subsequent return to this particular ministry

14. What choice/commitment is called for in the following passages?

    Romans 10:9-10, 13

    Colossians 3:16-17

    Titus 2:11-12

15. What commitment (if any) do you need to make today?

What hinders you from making it?

Growth Chart
16. Turn to the *Growth Chart* on page 95. Notice the first step is at the bottom of the page because a growth chart always reads from the bottom up. This week's Step, "Make That Commitment" is filled in to illustrate how the chart works. In succeeding weeks you will be asked to fill in the chart, one step per week. If you like to doodle, draw stick figures, or decorate the edges of your paper, try using your creativity to illustrate some of the steps on the chart.

❧ DIGEST ❧

Many years ago in one of our churches, a lay teacher came to my husband and asked, "Pastor, what am I doing wrong?" He proceeded to tell Ken how he had been leading a Bible study with a certain couple for six weeks or more. While the couple was eager for the study, there was no evidence of obedience to the Word. The study seemed to have made no impact upon their lives. In fact, the couple continued their involvement in a number of activities which were legally and morally questionable.

The discouraged teacher was sure that he was failing in his responsibility toward the couple. My husband assured him, "You are doing all that you can do—sowing the seed." Then he pointed out that until the couple made a commitment to Jesus Christ, there was nothing on which to build.

Choose to Obey
Obedience begins with a definite choice. It is not enough to determine "I'll try it and see if I like it." One must be willing to commit oneself to the process.

Hebrews 11:24-25 records Moses' choice. He relinquished his standing as the son of Pharaoh's daughter in order to identify himself with Pharaoh's slaves. Exodus 2 shows how deep was this commitment. Things didn't turn out the way Moses expected they would. Yet there is no indication that he ever regretted his decision.

Moses had lived in the palace for 40 years. Growing up as the adopted grandson of Pharaoh had afforded him every educational advantage available at the time. Egypt was the center of civilization. Whatever was to be learned, surely would be learned in Egypt. Thus Moses became skilled in word and deed while his fellow Hebrews became bitter and resigned to their lot. While he learned his lessons under the care of a tutor, they baked bricks under the whip of an overseer. For them, life consisted of long hours and hard labor. For him, there was luxury and security.

Then one day Moses, the slave who had become a prince, went for a walk in the brickyards. All the problems he had escaped for four decades suddenly became his as he saw sweating slaves harassed and tormented by the Egyptians. According to Stephen's sermon in Acts 7:25, Moses believed that God had sent him to deliver the slaves and he believed that the slaves would know that God had sent him. Thus, he immediately began his one-man "Help the Hebrews" campaign.

Of course he did not find things as he had expected. The slaves understood nothing about the plan. His crusade lasted about two days. On the first, Moses saw an Egyptian beating a slave. He intervened and in the fracas he killed the Egyptian. On the second day, to his dismay, he found two slaves quarreling. He reprimanded the one at fault.

To his surprise, the men both turned on him. "Who made you a prince and a judge over us?" they asked. "And what are you going to do, kill us like you killed the Egyptian?"

Their first question seems to indicate that they believed their self-appointed judge was a despised Egyptian inside Hebrew skin. One can well imagine that there were other questions implied here:

"Who needs you—you with your Egyptian ways and prince's robes?"

"What have you been doing all these years while we've been slaving away for the great Pharaoh?"

One thing was clear. Moses could not go home again. When the news of the slain Egyptian reached Pharaoh's ears, not even his adopted grandchild would escape the ruler's wrath. So ended Moses' brief crusade. In fear of his life, he ran away to Midian.

In the brickyards, nothing had changed. For Moses, nothing would ever again be the same.

In light of Moses' immediate failure, it is easy to overlook the importance of his commitment. In God's eyes, it was Moses' choice, not his attempted deliverance, that counted. His involvement in the brickyard was no mere humanitarian impulse. He gave up one thing in favor of another. And God called this choice an act of faith. "By faith Moses . . . refused to be known as the son of Pharaoh's daughter. He chose to be mistreated along with the people of God" (Heb. 11:24-25).

The Cost of Commitment
There was a cost to Moses' commitment. Overnight his lifestyle drastically changed. In Midian he traded his princely robes for shepherd's garb and spent the next four decades leading around a flock of sheep. There is no record of his looking back to his palace comforts with regret. That

fact presents an inescapable contrast between Moses and the people he ultimately delivered.

When the great Exodus came, the slaves were halfheartedly looking for a better life. When it failed to materialize immediately, they vacillated. The farther from Egypt they were removed, the better Egypt looked. They forgot the bondage and romanticized the past. In their hearts they constantly turned back to Egypt. They blamed Moses for every discomfort. "Why didn't you leave us alone? We want to go back!" Humanly speaking, those were complaints by a people who had left nothing, registered against a leader who had left everything. Yet the leader never once retaliated by saying, "Why did I ever leave the palace?"

Continuing Commitment Makes a Difference

When Moses refused to be called the son of Pharaoh's daughter and chose to suffer with his brethren, his decision was final. Whatever the future held, there was no turning back.

His commitment marked the first step of his long journey with God. Ultimately it made all the difference on that journey. It will make all the difference on your spiritual journey as well.

✿ *PERSONAL RESPONSE JOURNAL* ✿

1. Use this journal page to record any private thoughts you may have had concerning spiritual choices which currently confront you.
2. Write out a prayer to God in which you talk to Him about at least one of these choices.

_____

_____

_____

_____

_____

_____

_____

_____

_____

_____

_____

_____

_____

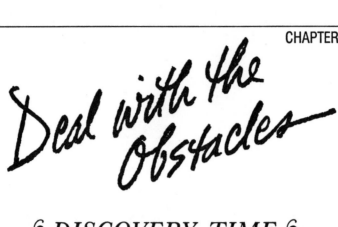

CHAPTER TWO

❧DISCOVERY TIME❧

Read Exodus 3:1–4:18.

1. Read the passage in one sitting, concentrating on the general facts of the incident. Close your eyes and try to mentally reconstruct what took place, recalling as many details as possible.

2. Moses was 80 years of age at the time of his encounter at the burning bush (See Acts 7:23-30). He had now lived in Midian for as long as he lived in Pharaoh's palace. What possible contrasts do you see between Moses' life as described here and his former life as the "son of Pharaoh's daughter"? (3:1)

3. From the following passages, summarize what God revealed to Moses at the burning bush.

Exodus 3:2-5

Exodus 3:6

Exodus 3:7-9

4. Summarize God's command, Moses' response, and God's promise in Exodus 3:10-12.

5. Follow the dialogues in Exodus 3:13-15; 4:1-4, 6, 9-13. What questions does Moses ask? What protests or arguments does he raise?

6. What was the purpose of the miraculous signs? (4:1, 5, 8-9)

7. Compare Exodus 2:13-14, 3:13, and 4:1. What clues do you find regarding the reasons for Moses' reluctance to obey.

8. In what way might Moses' 40 years as a shepherd following 40 years as a prince have prompted his response in Exodus 3:11, 4:13.

In what way might his response have been affected by his previous failure to deliver Israel?

9. Can you think of an incident from your own life where you were urged to do something you didn't want to do? What were your reasons? How did you handle it?

10. Rate the following potential obstacles to obedience. Give a 1 to the obstacle that holds the lowest potential, a 10 for highest, etc.

feeling of inadequacy

fear of failure

unspoken doubts (about self, God, the Word, etc.)

lack of commitment

other

11. Do you think believers are encouraged to be honest about these obstacles? Why or why not?

12. In what way are we sometimes pressured to ignore the existence of doubts?

Put Yourself in Moses' Sandals
13. Imagine that you have felt impressed that God wants you to do a certain task at which you have already failed miserably. You want to be obedient but you have unresolved questions. How would you express your questions, protests, arguments to the Lord? Write them out.

Growth Chart

14. *Growth Step: Deal with the obstacles.* Moses dealt with each obstacle to his obedience by looking for answers to his many questions and doubts. Copy this Growth Step on the Growth Chart on page 95. Think of a simple way to illustrate this step in the chart. For example, you might draw a big question mark or a series of small ones on the margin next to Growth Step #2.

❦ DIGEST ❧

"She doesn't know a thing about that organ." My cheeks reddened as I overheard the soloist commenting to her husband on my lack of skill. I knew that she did not mean to be unkind—she faced a very real dilemma. How could she sing with an accompanist who didn't know what she was doing?

Meanwhile I was struggling with my own dilemma. Once again I had been pressed into a service for which I was totally inadequate. My music training was minimal—less than a year of formal lessons altogether. Still, the fact that I played "a little organ," and "a little piano," often got me into situations where I was way over my head. Somehow I always felt as if I had to go along with whatever people demanded.

The soloist's remark, which was not intended for my ears, caused me to begin to deal more realistically with my own dilemma. I made some prayerful decisions as a result.

Facing Personal Inadequacy
At that stage of my life I was involved in several areas of ministry. I had no time, money, or inclination to pursue music lessons. Without such training I knew I would never be a "first choice" church musician. On the other hand, I reasoned that we must all at one time or another be willing to do things at which we are not very skilled. Thus I continued to "substitute for the substitute." However, I began to be much more bold in spelling out the limitations. "Yes, I will play for the congregation if I can approve the songs." "No, I will not accompany any soloist or choir." "No, I cannot serve as your regular instrumentalist."

Over the years I have met at least two women who faced my same dilemma and arrived at a totally different solution. Feeling that God would have them minister in this area, they set out to become proficient on the piano. They reviewed long-neglected childhood music training, resumed private lessons, substituted for the substitute, and eventually became accomplished church pianists.

Many times, reluctance to take on a certain task goes deeper than the question of adequate training. Often we grapple with more personal questions or, in some cases, doubts that refuse to go away.

"What if people don't accept me?"

"What if I fail?"

"I have so many doubts, I feel like a hypocrite."

Fear of Rejection

When God confronted Moses with a task, his first question was, "Who am I that I should go to Pharaoh?"

Who indeed? At 80 years of age he was a prince without a palace, a man without a country, and a shepherd without a flock. Not a very impressive resumé. Add to that the fact that for 40 years he had hardly talked to anyone other than all those sheep. Certainly he had not had any recent audiences with heads of state. No wonder he questioned whether he was the right choice to speak to Pharaoh. As for speaking to the Israelites, the only experience he had for that job was 40 years ago and had ended with his expulsion from Egypt.

God gently answered his questions, assuring him, "But of course, I'll be with you!" Today we are similarly reassured through the written Word, "My grace is sufficient for you, for My power is made perfect in weakness" (2 Corinthians 12:9).

Fear of Failure

Fear of failure is a common response to failure itself. "I've failed once, why try again?" Left alone, this fear can multiply rapidly, crippling those caught in its grip.

Several years ago I watched our oldest daughter maneuver our car over a treacherous winter road. A series of unexpected emergencies had placed upon her the responsibility of driving part of the family home from Lake Tahoe. Her driving experience under such conditions was limited, but she made the journey without incident and—thankful, tense and tired—fell into a hot bath.

It gave me cause to reflect on her very first driving experience. With learner's permit in hand, she climbed behind the wheel while I positioned myself in the passenger seat. Our journey ended before it hardly began as she plowed into the mailboxes, flattening the neighbor's box as well as ours.

When my husband came home an hour later, he immediately found our daughter, handed her the car keys and said, "Let's try again. The longer you put it off, the harder it will be to get behind the wheel again."

Facing the fear at once kept it from multiplying.

Moses had 40 years to live with his failure—40 years to wander the desert recalling every detail of his attempted deliverance; 40 years to wonder, "Where did I go wrong?"; 40 years to convince himself that he was not the man for the job. And then God spoke to him. Clearly, God wanted Moses to try again.

While at first glance the "burning bush" experience may appear to be a low point in Moses' faith, I see it as a valuable time of honest seeking. Moses dealt with every obstacle to his obedience openly and honestly. In time, we will see that this honesty paid off.

Dealing with Doubts

Most of us can relate to one or more of the questions Moses had as well as raise a few others. But many believers are conditioned to keep questions and doubts to themselves. We go about pretending all is well or hoping what we ignore will go away. But trying to function as a believer while concealing deeply hidden doubts can make one feel like a hypocrite.

What should we do with doubt?

My husband once preached on the subject giving the following suggestions on "What to do with your doubts."

Don't marry them. (Don't try to live with them.)

Don't bury them. (Don't try to ignore them.)

Don't carry them. (Don't try to deal with them alone.)

Deal with them. Face them in the light of God's Word. There is no doubt so great, no question so complicated, that it cannot be answered from the Word. Find a sympathetic, knowledgeable, spiritual mentor to help you examine the Scripture. Determine that you, like Moses, will persist in a dialogue with God until your questions and/or doubts are resolved.

❧ *PERSONAL RESPONSE JOURNAL* ❧

Thought Starter: Try writing a letter to God in which you acknowledge (1) your struggles with inadequacy or (2) other current obstacles to obedience.

_____

_____

_____

_____

_____

_____

_____

_____

_____

_____

_____

_____

CHAPTER THREE

Just Say Yes to God

🐾 *DISCOVERY TIME* 🐾

Read Exodus 4:14-20; 4:27–5:4.

1. From Exodus 4:27–5:4 list some specific areas in which Moses showed obedience.

2. Considering Moses' reluctance to obey, what significance do you see in Exodus 4:19-20?

   In what way does Moses provide a model for us today?

3. Compare Exodus 4:30-31 with 3:9-11. What contrast do you see between the Children of Israel's initial response to God's message and Moses' initial response at the burning bush?

   Drawing from your knowledge of the Exodus account, how important is the initial response in the big picture? Explain.

5. Compare Exodus 4:30-31 with 4:3-5. What do you think it means when it says the people "believed"? What did they believe? Why did they believe? How did they act upon this belief?

How do you think the people felt when they heard they were to be delivered from Pharaoh's tyranny? Use adverbs, adjectives.

6. Review Exodus 13:17-18; 14:1-12. What adjectives, adverbs would describe how Israel felt at this juncture?

7. What action did the Israelites take? (14:21-22)

8. How does God evaluate this action? (Hebrews 11:29)

What does this evaluation tell you about faith?

What does it tell you about obedience?

9. Is there anything about the Israelites that could provide a model for believers today? Explain.

10. In the following passages you will see two other biblical characters who were reluctant to obey God. Read the Scriptures and compare the characters to Moses by answering the questions below.

Judges 6:11-24
How did Gideon show his reluctance to obey God?

What similarities do you see between Gideon's encounter and Moses' encounter at the burning bush?

Judges 6:25-27
How would you characterize Gideon's obedience at this juncture?

Judges 6:34-40
In what ways does this passage indicate Gideon's reluctance to obey?

In what way does it indicate his willingness to obey?

Jonah 1:1-4, 11-12, 17.
How does Jonah's reluctance to obey contrast with Gideon's and Moses'?

What was the significant factor in Jonah's overcoming his reluctance to obey?

11. What was your biggest struggle with obedience as a child?

What have been your children's biggest struggles with obedience?

How is a pattern of obedience established?

12. What are some specific areas in which believers commonly struggle with obeying God?

13. Can you share with the group an experience in which something (or someone) has influenced you to obey the Lord?

14. Moses continued his dialogue with God as he struggled with his will, but he also obeyed even when he didn't want to. Specifically, how would believers follow this example today?

Put Yourself in Moses' Sandals

15. Imagine yourself in Moses' and Jonah's shoes. You often find yourself struggling with your will versus God's will. Will you follow Moses' example or Jonah's? It's your decision. In whose sandals would you rather be?

Growth Chart

16. *Growth Step: Say yes to God.* However reluctantly it is offered, obedience is a positive growth step and can lead to a more complete obedience. Copy this Growth Step on the Growth Chart on page 95.

❧ *DIGEST* ❧

As a potential obstacle to obedience, nothing surpasses the human will. Questions may be answered; arguments refuted; doubts erased; every reason for reluctance taken away.

Yet the will stubbornly refuses to obey God.

On the other hand, one may choose to obey God in spite of a lingering reluctance to do so.

Man's Will Versus God's Will

The Scriptures are full of examples of people who wrestled with their wills. Eve's struggle with Satan in the garden was largely a struggle with her own will. King Saul continually struggled with his will versus God's commands. Our Lord Himself, sweat great drops of blood as He struggled between His will and the will of the Father. In agony He prayed, "Not My will, but Yours be done" (Luke 22:42-43).

In this session, we have examined various examples of biblical characters who struggled with the question of man's will versus God's will. From each one we can draw some practical help for facing similar struggles.

Israel   Unlike the other examples, Israel showed no immediate reluctance to God's message. There was none of Moses' "How can I be sure of this?" attitude. There was none of Gideon's "Where have You been up till now?" The Israelites bowed their heads and worshiped God on the spot, apparently willing to accept His plan without a question.

But Israel floundered when the going got rough. They were terrified of Pharaoh's pursuing armies; they were angry at Moses for getting them into the situation; they wanted desperately to turn back the clock and subject themselves to Pharaoh once more. Only because God skillfully eliminated other options did they ultimately obey Him.

Jonah   Jonah is an example of deliberate disobedience. Clearly this man would sooner have died than given in to God's will. Given the opportunity to repent of his disobedience, he chose death beneath the raging water. But God did not allow him to escape so readily. He persistently pursued his disobedient servant. He prepared a fish to swallow him up, and Jonah was given one more chance to say yes to God.

Gideon Moses and Gideon differed from Jonah in that they did not deliberately disobey God. They differed from the Israelites in that they did not readily accept God's initial message.

The two men have this in common: each questioned God and openly talked to Him about all the things that made them reluctant to obey. Each obeyed in spite of his reluctance.

Reluctant Obedience Is a Start

In all these examples, we find that obedience came only after great struggles; yet three of the four are listed in Hebrews 11 as having acted in faith. We may conclude that God places a high priority on obedience, however reluctantly offered.

In Moses' case we see that reluctant obedience was a step that led to a greater, more complete obedience. For this reason, when wrestling with the will, a step of reluctant obedience can be the most important step for both the present and the future.

As a teenager, I struggled with God's will for my life. While I loved the Lord and wanted Him always to be a part of my life, I wanted to maintain control over that life. Already I had many plans—enough to last for half a century, and God did not figure closely in any of them.

Through the lessons I was learning at our weekly youth Bible study, the Lord continued to deal with me about my future. I struggled over college and career choices—my will versus what I felt very strongly was God's will.

For the most part it was a private struggle. While I argued with God over my future, I continued to be faithful in my commitment at our church. I studied assigned lessons and publicly responded as expected. But privately, I stubbornly reminded God of all the reasons why I could not change my plans.

A handful of believers, including my mother, were praying for me all the while, though none knew the depth of my struggles.

One summer Sunday evening, I sat in the sanctuary listening to a missionary speaker. I cannot recall who he was, where he was from, or what he said. But at the end of the message I knew I could no longer pit my will against God's will. In response to the invitation to "dedicate oneself to full-time Christian service," I walked forward. Significantly, I was not rejoicing but I did have peace as I prayed, "Lord, I don't want to do this, but if it's what You want, I will do it."

That reluctant step was a beginning. My career plans, my choice of college all changed. I went on to graduate from a Christian college and later served a year under a home mission board in the Ozark Mountains. Today I continue to serve Him as a pastor's wife, a writer, and a speaker.

There have been many important steps of obedience which have brought me to this juncture in my life, but none have been so crucial as that first step. Reluctant obedience is such a little thing to offer God. Yet if that's all you have to offer, offer Him that. It is enough. It is a beginning.

❧PERSONAL RESPONSE JOURNAL❧

Thought Starter: Are you willing to just say yes to God? Can you tell Him, "Lord, even though I don't want to _____, if that's what You want, I will do it"?

_____

_____

_____

_____

_____

_____

_____

_____

_____

_____

_____

CHAPTER FOUR

Keep on Keeping On

❧ DISCOVERY TIME ❧

Read Exodus 5:5–6:13.

1. What was Pharaoh's immediate reaction to Moses' and Aaron's request? (5:5-9)

What action did he take?

What reasons did he give for his actions?

2. Egyptian slave drivers were in charge in the brickyards. In the operational organization they used Hebrew slaves as foremen over the other slaves. Pharaoh's decree affected both levels—the Hebrew foremen and the common slaves (5:9-14).

How did Pharaoh's decree affect the common slaves?

How did it affect the Hebrew foremen?

Who suffered the most severely from Pharaoh's order? Explain.

3. What course of action did the Hebrew foremen take? (5:15-16)

How would you characterize the foremen's presentation to Pharaoh?

4. Do you think the officers were surprised at Pharaoh's response? Why or why not? (5:17-21)

5. What do you think was the rationale behind their accusation against Moses and Aaron? (5:19-21)

6. To whom did Moses take his questions and complaints? (5:22-23)

Find at least two questions and at least two accusatory statements in this passage. Write them out.

7. What do you think discouraged Moses the most about the situation? Explain.

8. Had you been in Moses' situation, what would have most likely disillusioned you?

9. How would you characterize God's reply to Moses? (6:1-8)

   How many times does the pronoun *I* (God speaking) occur in this passage? What significance do you see in this, if any?

   What part of God's answer was Moses to repeat to the Israelites?

10. Explain how disillusionment effected various responses (6:9-12).

    How do you think Moses felt at this juncture about:

His future?

His task?

The lack of fruit from his obedience?

How well do you think he heard/understood the promises God continued to make to him?

11. In what way did God encourage Moses for the task? (7:1-6)

In what way did He forewarn him of the difficulty of the task?

In what way did He explain to Moses what He was about?

12. In light of Moses' disillusionment, what significance do you see in Exodus 7:6?

Put Yourself in Moses' Sandals

13. After months of struggling over a decision, you have reluctantly accepted a position believing that God would have you involved in a certain ministry. While not confident that you have the skills, you wholeheartedly throw yourself into the work. After two weeks, it becomes apparent that:

☐ An already bad situation has worsened;
☐ The people to whom you minister blame you;
☐ You see no evidence that God is taking your sacrificial labor and turning it into something productive.

How would you feel?

What would you say to God?

What choices might you make?

Growth Chart

14. *Growth Step: Obey God without regard to circumstances.* As we offer God our obedient service, we, like Moses, are sometimes confronted with disillusionment. His example challenges us to exercise obedience amid disillusioning circumstances. Copy this Growth Step on the Growth Chart on page 95.

DIGEST

The late Dr. V. Raymond Edman wrote a classic devotional book, *The Disciplines of Life,* in which he notes that disillusionment wrecks our equilibrium of spirit. In other words, disillusionment throws our spirit off balance. We see all our undertakings as having no purpose. We look at them and ask ourselves, "What's the use?"

"I did my part, why did God let me down?" demands the disillusioned parent. "I've worked hard for God all my life, is this the way He rewards me?" questions a young woman suffering from a disfiguring disease. "I've given 10 years of my life to this church, but when I needed help, no one lifted a finger," laments a hard working volunteer in a "caring church."

Cost-Effective Obedience Sets Us Up for Disillusionment
In my book, *Is There Life After Johnny?* (Here's Life Publishers), I made this statement concerning parental disillusionment: "Disillusionment is sometimes born in the simple act of doing all the right things for all the wrong reasons." Whether in our parenting efforts or in other areas of life, we set ourselves up for disillusionment by our "cost-effective" attitude toward our task.

The mother who raises her children by a biblical standard expects to be rewarded by wise and obedient children.

The young woman who gives sacrificially of her time in doing battle for the Lord expects to be rewarded with the blessing of good health.

The volunteer who spends years serving the Lord by meeting the needs of the body of Christ, expects to be rewarded in kind when the occasion calls for it.

While each purposes to do a good thing for the Lord, consciously or unconsciously each expects something in return. "I'll do this for God and then He will do that for me." When subsequently faced with uncontrollable offspring, disease of the body, or inconsiderate fellow believers, they become disillusioned, crying out, "What's the use?" or, in some cases, "God has let me down."

Moses' Expectations

From the conversation in Exodus 5:22-23, we see that Moses was disillusioned. Obviously he had expected more of God. And why not? After all, he had obediently followed God even when he didn't want to. Shouldn't God at least bring something good out of such "sacrificial obedience"?

He didn't.

Moses' obedience produced nothing positive. Things got worse instead of better.

So Moses asked God, "Why am I here, and what are you doing?"

No Escape

My youngest daughter once presented me with a poster showing Charles Schulz's lovable Linus dragging his blanket. The caption reads: "No problem is so big or so complicated that it can't be run away from!" We have laughed a lot over that poster because there are so many times when it seems as if Linus has the right idea!

In the real world, however, escape is seldom the solution to either the disillusionment or the circumstances which produce it. As it was with Moses, so it is with believers today—along with God's encouragement often comes God's directive: "Continue on!"

No Explanation

Like Moses, we often demand explanations for our circumstances. "Why are You doing this, God?" "Why have You sent me here?" We tend to think, *If I could only understand, I could accept my situation a lot easier.*

Note that while God patiently responded to Moses' questions, He did not explain. Instead, in a dialogue crammed with promises, He reminded Moses that He would take care of everything (Exodus 6:1-8). What Moses needed most was not an explanation, but a change of perspective. He needed to divert his eyes from his situation long enough to focus on the promises God continually made to him. So long as Moses' eyes were on circumstances, his heart would continue to cry, "Why?"

Perhaps you are going through difficult circumstances which you do not understand. Perhaps you, like Moses, are asking God, "Why me? Why this? Why now?"

Reminding yourself of God's promises is no magic key to changing your circumstances (or making you feel better about them), but it is a way to focus on God and on your commitment to obey Him.

Obey and Trust

"Cheer up, things could be worse," is a trite way of dealing with disillusioning circumstances. One wit comments on this, "So I cheered up, and sure enough things got worse."

After God reassured Moses that He was going to take care of everything, He commanded him to speak to the Israelites once again. In spite of his disillusionment, Moses obeyed.

Now that was a good sign. To obey under such conditions was no small offering to God. Surely He would reward Moses this time with a positive response from an eager audience. He didn't.

The children of Israel were so discouraged over the latest development in the brickyard that they refused to listen to Moses. Understandably, Moses began to see the whole plan as hopeless. Thus, when God told him to go to Pharaoh, Moses argued, "If the Israelites won't even listen, why should Pharaoh listen?" He had a point. The Israelites were the designated winners in the Exodus, and Pharaoh was set to lose all his manpower.

In spite of his mental and emotional state—in spite of the fact that he couldn't understand what God was doing, Moses once again obeyed. He went to speak to Pharaoh.

Continued obedience is the believer's responsibility—even when it appears to be "all for nothing." We don't have to understand what God is about. We do have to obey—and trust Him.

No Alternative To Obedience

From this very negative time of Moses' life, we find two helpful examples: (1) he never stopped talking to God and (2) he continued to obey God, even when he felt his efforts were without purpose.

How easily we are drawn into "cost-effective" obedience. "God, I didn't want to do this. But I did it because You demanded it of me. I fully expected that You would accept such sacrificial obedience and turn it into something productive." However sacrificially it may be offered, there will be times when our obedience appears to be "unproductive." Disillusionment descends like a great wet blanket. At such times, the most dedicated believer is apt to cry out, "Why am I here? Where did I go wrong? How could I have been so sure that God was in this? If I could only understand, I could get through anything!"

Like Moses, we each must learn that our obedience is not linked to a set of circumstances. Rather it must be linked to a relationship with God. When we love Him, we want to obey Him. Our goal should be to make our obedience constant—even amid the most disillusioning circumstances.

❦ PERSONAL RESPONSE JOURNAL ❦

Thought Starter: Write any private thoughts or feelings you may have as a result of today's lesson. Write a prayer to God regarding any decisions you need to make.

_____

_____

_____

_____

_____

_____

_____

_____

_____

_____

_____

_____

CHAPTER FIVE

Leave the Results to God

❧ DISCOVERY TIME ❧

Scan Exodus 7–10.

1. Review Exodus 7:1-2 and compare it with 4:15-16. What chain of command do you find in this passage?

   What was the specific task of each person in the chain?

2. Who was giving orders in Exodus 7:14-19?

   What was Moses' responsibility?

   How did Aaron fit into the plan?

   What part of the message confronted Pharaoh's stubbornness?

What part of the message explained God's purpose to Pharaoh?

3. In what way did Moses and Aaron demonstrate obedience in Exodus 7:20-25?

Did this obedience result in a positive change of the situation? Explain.

4. What similarities do you see in Exodus 8:1-8 with the preceding plague?

What happened for the first time here?

5. Analyze the conversation in Exodus 8:8-15 and answer the following:

Who called for confrontation?

For what reason?

Why do you think Moses was willing to have Pharaoh determine the time of deliverance from frogs?

What was the end result of this plague?

6. What are the similarities of the plague described in Exodus 8:16-19 with the previous two?

What are the differences?

What effect did this plague have?

7. What new development is seen with the judgment of the flies? (Exodus 8:20-24)

What was God's purpose in it?

8. What warning does Moses give to Pharaoh? (Exodus 8:25-32)

What do you think might have been going through Moses' mind at this time?

9. What evidence did Pharaoh seek? (Exodus 9:1-7)

What effect did it have on him?

10. Review Exodus 9:13-26 carefully. Note God's warning to Pharaoh. Write out the phrase that explains God's purpose in the plagues.

What does God have to say about the power of God and people with power?

11. Compare Exodus 9:27-35 with 5:23, 8:29, 9:29-30. In what way has Moses experienced a change of attitude?

What do you think was his perspective on responsibility for the task in 5:23?

What was it in 9:29-30?

Put Yourself in Moses' Sandals

12. Moses obviously felt a great responsibility to be successful in the task
    to which God had called him—so much so that he failed to recog-
    nize that God was taking responsibility for the success of His divine
    plan. Through the experience of the plagues he gained a new
    perspective on his task. He obeyed completely and left the results to
    God. What can you learn from Moses' experience to help you this
    week?

Growth Chart

13. *Growth Step: Leave the results to God.* Periodically, we must remind
    ourselves to surrender any self-imposed responsibility for success,
    obey God completely, and leave the results to Him. Copy this
    Growth Step on the Growth Chart on page 95.

❧ *DIGEST* ❧

Most women want to succeed, no matter what hat they choose to wear—
  wife
    mother
      career woman
        —or all three.

Daily, we are confronted with a constant barrage of articles, books, and seminar opportunities designed to guarantee success.

A quick flip through this week's women's magazines or a walk through your favorite bookstore is sure to uncover the latest thoughts on how to be the ideal woman; how to function at your peak in your career; how to balance career with home; how to successfully "have it all."

Measuring Success

This can be a problem. Many times success is recognized not by what efforts you put out, but by what response those efforts produce.

If you are a leader, your success is measured by your followers. How many? What kind?

If you are a mother, your success is often measured by the behavior of your children.

If you are a teacher, your success is measured by the response of your pupils.

If you are a wife, your degree of success may be measured by how content your husband appears and how others perceive your marriage.

In short, success is measured by your influence—or lack of influence—on others. But the extent of your influence is sometimes an unknown factor. It may be years before the impact of your influence will be felt.

One Woman's Influence

My friend Lillian tells the story of her mother's influence on one small girl—the full impact of which was unknown until after her mother's death. When Lillian was small her parents spent a summer traveling from place to place, conducting daily vacation Bible schools coupled with evening evangelistic services. Lillian recalls one very discouraging time when they spent two weeks in one place, ministering every day and every night. At the end of the time, the offering netted $7.50, not nearly enough to feed the Olson family of six. Mrs. Olson was discouraged and ready to cancel the next school. But Mr. Olson believed that they should honor the commitment and proceed as scheduled. And so they went on to the next school and after that a Bible camp. It was a discouraging, dismal experience in many ways. They had miserable weather, no finances, and few responses to report for their summer's labor.

But there was one eleven-year-old girl who came to know the Lord through the Olsons' ministry. While visiting her grandmother who lived in the community, this young girl attended the vacation Bible school and memorized all the assigned Scriptures, earning a camp scholarship in the process. Although she was too young for camp, she was allowed to attend on the condition that Mrs. Olson assume responsibility for her. That week, with Mrs. Olson's help, the young camper put her faith and trust in Jesus Christ as her Savior.

Years later, after her mother died, Lillian discovered how far-reaching had been the impact of this one contact. A single young youth pastor joined the pastoral staff where Lillian's husband served as senior pastor. The youth pastor's parents had served for many years in Brazil heading a child evangelism ministry. When his mother came for a visit, Lillian invited her over for coffee. As they sat visiting, Lillian asked, "Why don't you share your testimony with me?" Imagine her surprise when she learned that this woman was the eleven-year-old girl whom her mother had pointed to Jesus so many years before. They cried afterward as Lillian told her of how her mother had been so discouraged she had wanted to give up. She had remained faithful to the task even when she could not see all that God was accomplishing in His plan.

The Need to Succeed
We saw in the last session how Moses' lack of visible influence upon Israel or Pharaoh had been a source of discouragement. His sense of responsibility for success is demonstrated as he calls on the Lord, "Why have You brought me here? Ever since I came in Your name, things have gotten worse, and You haven't even delivered these people. If the Children of Israel won't listen to me, why should Pharaoh listen?"

Exodus 7:4-5 records God's response to Moses' questions. It was at this point that God told Moses He would deliver the Israelites by great judgments—"and the Egyptians shall know that I am the Lord." There was a purpose in the delay after all. Israel's release was to be forced through a plan which would be a learning experience for Egypt. Clearly, the plan also proved to be a learning experience for Moses.

Surrendering Self-Imposed Responsibility for Success

Through the experience of the plagues, we see Moses going through an important metamorphosis. As God works His daily miracles under the very nose of the mighty Pharaoh, Moses has a change of perspective. No longer does he appear to be concerned about circumstances or bewildered because God hasn't changed those circumstances. No longer does he question what God is about. He looks Pharaoh in the eye and declares, "I will pray and God will take away the hail, but as for you, I know you won't do as you promised."

It no longer mattered to Moses that he didn't know what was coming next. He just followed instructions . . . and watched.

As Moses spoke, God turned the river to blood. Frogs infested the land. Dust became living, crawling lice. Flies swarmed over Egypt. Disease destroyed the livestock. Boils broke out on man and beast. Hail destroyed the crops. Locusts stripped away what was left. Thick black darkness enshrouded Pharaoh's kingdom. Clearly, God was in control here, even if the Israelites were still in bondage.

Moses has learned an important lesson—God is in control of the plan and Moses is but His instrument. At last he understands that God has called him to obedience, not to success.

Do you sometimes feel overburdened with the responsibility of some personal ministry? Do you too easily assume that obedience only counts when it produces some visible positive response?

A young single friend sat in my living room pouring her heart out about her inability to help a friend who was facing difficult times. In part, these difficulties were self-imposed, and my friend had lovingly pointed out some things that needed to be dealt with. But her counsel was refused. Now she felt like a failure.

"In what way have you failed?" I asked.

"I don't know. I just feel like I ought to be able to fix everything."

At times we look at the choices people make and feel that their lack of response to our ministry somehow diminishes the validity of our endeavors. Yet, we cannot force the will of those we hope to influence. Each man, woman, and child makes his or her own choice.

More than once, Moses questioned the value of his efforts because the Israelites failed to respond positively. He came to a turning point in his life when he surrendered his self-imposed responsibility for success and concentrated on obedience.

Called to Be Instruments

Certainly there are areas in every woman's life in which she may legitimately set success-oriented goals. She may measure her success by her progress toward those goals. But when it comes to obedience and ministry, we must learn by Moses' example. We are called to obedience, not to success. We are but instruments in God's hand.

To fully understand this, it is important to recognize that an instrument has no success apart from the hand that wields it. Thus the responsibility for success belongs not to the instrument, but to the hand.

❧ *PERSONAL RESPONSE JOURNAL* ❧

Thought Starter: Write any thoughts you may have on your own struggle with the pressure to succeed.

_____

_____

_____

_____

_____

_____

_____

_____

_____

_____

_____

CHAPTER SIX

Get a Perspective on the Promises

❦ DISCOVERY TIME ❦

Read Exodus 11:1-10; 12:1-12.

1. Compare Exodus 11:3 with 2:14; 4:1, 10, 13. What did God accomplish for Moses through the execution of the plagues?

2. What specific facts do you learn about the judgment in Exodus 11:1-10?

   v. 1

   vv. 4-6

   v. 7

   v. 8

v. 9

3. In Exodus 12:1-12 God gives His instructions for future commemorations of their deliverance from Egypt. What do you learn about the preparation from the following passages?

   12:1-5

   12:6-7

   12:8-11

4. According to verse 12, who was the target of this final judgment?

5. What do you understand to be the purpose of the Passover feast? (Exodus 12:21-28)

   From what is the name derived?

6. What were the Israelites celebrating at the first Passover?

Where was this first Passover observed?

What significance do you see in this?

7. Read Hebrews 11:28. Notice that the word *kept* in this passage means instigated. Why do you think God called this an act of faith on Moses' part?

8. God asked Moses to plan a celebration commemorating a deliverance which has not yet taken place. What does his obedience at this point tell you about Moses' attitude toward God's commands?

What does it tell you about his attitude toward God's promises?

9. In what way do you think Moses has changed since he met God at the burning bush? (See Exodus 3–4.)

How do you think the change occurred?

10. In what way was God's word proved in the passages below?

    Exodus 12:29-36

    Exodus 12:40-42 (See Genesis 15:13.)

11. Compare Hebrews 11:29 with Exodus 14:10-12, 15-16, 22. What did God say about the Israelites in the first passage?

    What adjectives or adverbs best describe the Israelites' feelings or attitudes at the time they faced the Red Sea crossing?

    What positive statement could you make about the Israelites at this juncture?

    In what way does the contrast of these passages add to your understanding of faith?

Put Yourself in Moses' Sandals

12. At this point in his relationship with God, Moses had at last begun to perceive the promises of God as accomplished facts. Such confidence allowed him to act upon those promises, obeying more readily than before.

    Imagine that you are the old Moses—the one before the plagues. God has asked you to celebrate the promised deliverance. How might you have responded? Write out what you would have said.

Growth Chart

13. *Growth Step: Accept God's promises as accomplished facts.* While this is the point at which we often assume every believer should begin, remember Moses went through a growing period before he could accept God's promises so readily. Review the steps on the Growth Chart on page 95 and then fill in today's Growth Step.

❧ DIGEST ❧

Two entries in the guest log at a U.S. Forest Service station provide some interesting comments on a group backpacking experience. In the first entry, a female hiker recalled details of the grueling trip: "My blisters have blisters, the mosquitoes were huge, the days were unbearably hot, we froze every night. This has been a terrible experience. JoAnn."

The second entry provided a different version of the same hike. Brief and to the point, a hiker named Mike, wrote, "It was an incredible trip. We had a wonderful time—except for JoAnn."

Perspective Makes a Difference
The same set of circumstances viewed from two different perspectives can produce altogether different responses. It is not hard to trace Moses' change of perspective. In the beginning he saw only the past failures and the lack of results. When circumstances did not change, he found reason to doubt God's words to him. By the time we arrive at the celebration of the first Passover, a new Moses has emerged. Circumstances have not altered. In spite of God's mighty display of power through nine judgments, the Israelites are still slaves. But Moses does not question or argue. He stands poised and waiting for each word from God. He readily obeys and watches expectantly for God's next move.

I doubt the old Moses would have celebrated deliverance from Egypt while they were still in Egypt—at least not without an argument. He would have contended that there would be time for celebration when the promised deliverance became reality. But with his new perspective, Moses understood that whatever God has promised is as good as done. So he instigated the Passover feast to commemorate their deliverance.

Ever since the time of the great Exodus, Jews all over the world have continued to commemorate that deliverance through the annual passover feast. There is one great difference between the very first Passover and all the ones that have followed—the first Passover was celebrated to commemorate an event that had not yet taken place. That's a little like celebrating an armistice before the war is over.

Still, from Moses' new perspective, there was nothing unusual about it. God said, "This night have I delivered thee." Moses saw God's promise as an accomplished fact. There was nothing left to do except celebrate!

Learn from Moses

Obviously between the burning bush experience and the last night in Egypt, a change took place in Moses' heart. What caused the change? What can we learn from his experience?

First, through all his doubting, discouragement, and disillusionment, Moses continued to obey God. Many times he didn't feel like it and many times he was sure it was to no purpose, but he obeyed, nevertheless.

Sometimes we face discouraging personal circumstances. It may be impossible to divert our minds completely away from them, but we must focus on being obedient, no matter what the circumstances.

Second, he never stopped talking to God. Throughout his experience, he cried out to God and listened to what God had to say. Many times Moses' heart didn't really hear, but he persisted in his dialogue with God.

Reading God's Word is our way of listening to God. This is crucial for a growing obedience. It may seem like a futile exercise at times, but persistence pays off. Persistence produces a wider knowledge, a better understanding, and a more accurate personal application of the Scriptures.

Third, as Moses continued to obey and to talk with God, he came to see that God's promises are not altered by circumstances. He caught a new glimpse of this God he served. With his eyes firmly focused on his God, he no longer cowered in the face of circumstances.

At times you may be less interested in God than in what He is doing— or not doing—in the circumstances of your life. Remember what brought Moses to his new perspective. He continued in obedience and in his daily dialogue with God.

In this session there are three important areas of consideration for contemporary believers: the Passover, the faith of Israel, and the faith of Moses. The latter two are noted in Hebrews 11.

The Passover

The passover holds great significance for Christians as well as Jews for it foreshadows the death of Jesus Christ, the Lamb of God. A short while before His crucifixion, Jesus ate the Passover feast with His disciples.

Breaking the bread with them, He proclaimed, "This is My body, broken for you." As He held the wine, He said, "This is My blood shed for the remission of sins." In going to the Cross, He became the ultimate sacrifice for our sin.

It is through His death, burial, and resurrection that we have deliverance from sin and its consequences. Accepting His promise of salvation to all who believe on Him is the beginning. A growing obedience will follow if you, like Moses, continue in the Word, and continue to obey whether you want to or not.

Israel's Faith

Given the history of Israel's passage from Egypt to Canaan, it is somewhat surprising to discover that they are commended for acting in faith as they crossed the Red Sea (Hebrews 11:29). A glance at the record of this crossing (Exodus 14:10-12) reveals anything but faith as we usually define it. The Israelites were terrified when they came to the edge of the sea. They wanted to turn back. They complained that Moses had brought them out against their will.

Yet they did obey. In spite of their terror they crossed the sea as God had commanded. God counted that obedience for faith.

Once across, they sang a song of praise and thanksgiving for their deliverance. It was a good beginning, but it was downhill all the way after that. Their bent toward disobedience grew in stark contrast to Moses' ever growing obedience.

Acts 7:39 gives us a clue to Israel's problem with disobedience. Here, the martyr Stephen declares that Israel turned back in their hearts to Egypt. Each time the going got rough, they wished for Egypt. In time they looked upon Egypt as a land flowing with milk and honey, instead of the place of bondage it had been.

Their example provides both a positive and a negative lesson. From their experience we see that God puts a high priority on obedience, counting the most rudimentary obedience as an act of faith.

We also see that a growing obedience is impossible when the heart continually longs for the past with all the bondage that it represents.

Moses' Faith

This is noted in Hebrews 11:27-28, where Moses is commended for acting in faith as he forsook Egypt and instigated the passover feast. While it is true that all Israel kept the feast, it was Moses, acting in faith, who instigated the celebration. Having come to the understanding that God's word was sure and trustworthy, he readily acted upon that word.

If you would grow in your faith, keep in mind an important contrast between Moses and the Israelites. The Israelites were commended for crossing the Red Sea, but only Moses was commended for forsaking Egypt.

In the Hebrews passage, the forsaking of Egypt is directly tied to his instigation of the Passover celebration. After all the questions, doubts and arguments, after all the obeying when he didn't want to, Moses comes to a new juncture. He stands in Egypt's brickyards and sees the same old circumstances. The Hebrews are still slaves, and Pharaoh is as stubborn as ever. Only one thing is different. God said, "You're free. Celebrate!" Moses believed the promise and acted upon it.

Trusting His Promises Today

In our complicated society, women often face hard circumstances which seem to dictate that they ignore God's commands because they cannot believe His promises. Like Sarah of old, it seems God needs a little help in order to fulfill those promises.

Carol's Christian husband left her for another woman. Suddenly Carol found herself with two small children, another on the way, no home, and no means of support. Later, Carol met a kind and loving man who took her and her children in. From the beginning she said, "I know it's wrong and I'm living in sin, but I don't feel like I have a choice." Circumstances made it too difficult for her to trust God's promise of provision.

Don't let circumstances rob you of the joy of trusting God. Believe God and act accordingly. Wait expectantly on Him for He will fulfill that which He has promised.

❦ *PERSONAL RESPONSE JOURNAL* ❦

Thought Starter: Write out your thoughts on any area in which you need to trust God more.

_____

_____

_____

_____

_____

_____

_____

_____

_____

_____

_____

_____

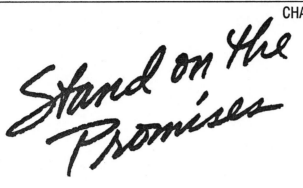

CHAPTER SEVEN

❦ *DISCOVERY TIME* ❦

Read Exodus 32.

1. Describe the scene in Exodus 31:18–32:6. Position Moses, Aaron, and the Israelites.

2. Compare Exodus 32:1-4 with 4:14-16, 27-31. What were Aaron's strong points?

What were his weak points?

What do you understand his "potential" for leadership to be?

On what did that leadership depend?

3. What charges does God make against Israel? (32:7-10)

How does He characterize the people?

What action does He declare He will take against them?

What promise does He make to Moses?

4. Carefully compare Exodus 32:11-14 with 6:1-8. What might lead us to believe that Moses' boldness on the mountain is based upon the promises of God?

5. What do you think went through Moses' mind as he came down from the mountain and entered the camp? (32:15-20)

Do you think seeing the event affected him more than hearing about it on the mountain top? Why or why not?

If you were in Moses' shoes at a point like this, how would you assess the following?

Your "right-hand man"

Your "following among the masses"

Your resources for getting your job done

6. How would you characterize Moses as a leader in this passage? (32:21-24)

7. In Exodus 32:25-33 we see a great contrast between Moses as judge and Moses as intercessor. Divide the passage according to the two roles.

Why do you think judgment was necessary?

What do we learn about Moses from the prayer?

8. What is different about God's charge to Moses in Exodus 32:34–33:3 as compared to previous charges (see 6:6-8).

9. How did the new proclamation affect the people? (33:4-10)

10. From the following passages discover the factors Moses could previously count on to make his task easier.

    Exodus 4:16

    Exodus 4:31

    Exodus 6:6-8

    Which of those now remain?

11. How would you describe Moses' approach to God in this passage? (33:12-17)

    In what way does the passage show Moses "standing on the promises"?

    Which verses best demonstrate his boldness?

On what do you think that boldness was based?

12. What have you learned from this lesson that would help you "stand on the promises of God"?

Put Yourself in Moses' Sandals

13. You are in a situation where you have been stripped of all resources other than the promises of God. What three promises would you stand on? Give references and explain.

Growth Chart

14. *Growth Step: Standing on the promises.* Moses was in a continuing dialogue with the Lord for a long period of time before he came to this level of obedience. We can have a continuing dialogue through reading the written Word of God regularly. Copy this session's Growth Step on the Growth Chart on page 95.

🍂 *DIGEST* 🍂

Shortly after her fourth birthday, our granddaughter Chelsie walked up to her mother with her new doll in her arms and said, "My baby is four years old today." Her mother replied, "She looks awfully little to be four." Chelsie immediately answered, "She's going to do a lot of growing up in the next 15 minutes."

Most of us can remember times when we had to do a lot of growing up in a short period of time. Stretching periods of life are often tied to sudden confrontations with reality. Facing reality means seeing a situation for what it is—being unable to deny its existence, realizing that "wishing" is not going to make it go away. Facing reality is asking, "Where do I go from here?"

Assess Resources

Katherine was faced with a "Where do I go from here?" situation when certain resources she had depended upon were taken from her. Her husband died quite suddenly within a few years after they had purchased their new, but modest home. She had two children at home. The loss of her husband meant loss of the chief breadwinner as well as loss of companionship.

Katherine also discovered that there was no mortgage insurance on the home. She had always assumed that if needed, she would have that security. She had counted on this resource when in fact, it was nonexistent.

Although Katherine faced a multiple loss of resources, she did have a marketable skill, good health, and most importantly—the Lord. Facing reality, assessing her few resources, helped Katherine to depend upon the Lord in a new way.

In Exodus 32–34, we have a vivid account of Moses confronting reality, assessing his resources, and making some important decisions. In preceding passages, we see Moses going up the mountain to talk with

God, leaving behind a relatively encouraging situation. There were positive signs in Israel. When confronted with God's promise to care for them if they would obey Him, the people had promised to do whatever God commanded.

In addition, Moses left Aaron, knowing that God had sent this brother to act as a spokesman. Everything seemed to be proceeding smoothly as he went up the mountain to continue receiving the Law from God.

He had spent more than a month talking to God on the mountain, when in the midst of the conversation, God informed him it was time to get back down to the camp because the people were worshiping a golden calf.

"They have already turned away from My commandments," God declared. He called them a stubborn people and declared that He would immediately destroy them and make a new nation out of Moses.

A close examination of the conversation in Exodus 32:7-13 shows that Moses is reminding God of promises He had previously made. (See verses 11-13.) The promises of God proved to be his most important asset.

God Remains Faithful

When Moses came down from the mountain, he came face to face with reality. The thunder of dancing feet and drunken voices silenced any hope he may have held that the people would learn to trust God. How could you expect a significant change in a people who, having witnessed so many miracles, would give deliberate obeisance to a metal monster?

As for Aaron, how much help could he be when he had so easily crumbled in the crisis, had in fact fashioned the golden calf they worshiped?

Perhaps we are never so dependent upon the Lord as when we are faced with the knowledge that all human help is gone. A young pastor's wife tells of a situation in which they found themselves.

"Even if someone wanted to help, there is nothing humanly speaking that anyone can do," she said. "We know that the only help we can hope for is whatever help the Lord chooses to give us."

Her husband was quick to add, "It's a matter of assessing our resources. In our situation, we have no place else to go."

This is the perspective that Moses seems to have as he continues his dialogue with God after coming down from the mountain. After judging the people's sin, he prays for God to forgive them, and then in an incredible conversation, boldly uses the one asset that remains—the promises of God.

Stand on the Promises

Although God has commanded Moses to proceed and lead the people to the land, Moses is not yet ready to go, because God declared, "I will send an angel before you and drive out the enemy, but I will not go with you—you are a stubborn people and I might consume you in the way." Since this is a reversal of a prior promise, Moses refuses to consider the issue closed.

Boldly, he approaches God and reopens the dialogue. "Look, You tell me 'Bring the people up,' but You haven't told me who is going with me."

At length God assures him, "I will go with you and I will give you rest." In his boldest reminder of God's promises, Moses declares, "If You're not going, Lord, don't send me."

There was something incredibly clear about Moses' perspective at that point. There was absolutely no confusion about resources, responsibilities, or relationships. Neither bravado nor audacity inspired him to communicate with God in that manner. Rather he was motivated by a frank assessment of his task and his position. He understood the immensity of his job. He knew precisely what was expected of him. He knew he was devoid of human resources. There was nothing left but the promises of God.

To stand upon God's promises we do not need to increase in boldness so much as we need to increase in the knowledge of God's promises. The more we familiarize ourselves with His Word, the more we understand the promises He has given. In times of need, we may boldly stand on those promises.

Several months ago I spoke at a weekend conference not far from the small town where I lived as a child. Not surprisingly, I met a number of women "from my past." As I visited with the young, attractive emcee, I discovered that I had known her mother. Immediately I began naming all her aunts and uncles, asking about them, even identifying their chronological birth order in the family of eight children. The emcee found it amazing that after more than three decades I remembered such details about her mother's family.

"Your mother's younger sister was one of my best friends at our church," I explained, "but, in any case, no one could forget that family. They were a family of orphans who took care of each other."

I met them shortly before their mother died. (The father had already died.) When the mother died, only the oldest son had married. Seven children remained at home. The youngest was perhaps eight years of age and my friend, the youngest girl, was probably ten.

She was sad at times, missing her mother, but more than once she said, "We have each other, and we have the Lord." Her parents had left them with few material resources, but they had given them a godly heritage. From their earliest memories these children had memorized the promises of God. In a time of crisis, they learned to stand on those promises.

When Moses came down from the mountain he made an important assessment. He had nothing left but the promises of God. He needed nothing more. He would settle for nothing less.

❧ PERSONAL RESPONSE JOURNAL ❧

Thought Starter: Can you write a prayer of praise to God that He has kept some specific promise? Or do you need to ask for courage as you attempt to stand on His promises?

_____

_____

_____

_____

_____

_____

_____

_____

_____

_____

_____

_____

CHAPTER EIGHT

&DISCOVERY TIME&

Read Numbers 10:33–11:35.

1. When Israel came to Sinai, shortly after their deliverance from Egypt, God began to prepare them for a new life as His chosen nation. The preservation of the people depended upon their obedience to Him as He told them how to organize; how to live under sanitary conditions; how to rule fairly; and how to worship the God who was leading them. This preparation was interrupted by the incident of the golden calf. Following that incident, we see Moses once again taking care of the many details necessitated by his position as God's leader. From the following passages, discover some of the things which took place while Israel camped at Sinai.

Exodus 34:1-4, 28

Exodus 34:31-32

Exodus 39:33; 40:1-2

Numbers 1:1-3

Numbers 9:1-5

2. Scan Numbers 10:13-28. Here the Israelites were given the order in which they would march when on the move. In order to move such a large group of people it was necessary to maintain precise order in the marching ranks.

3. In Numbers 10:33-36 the Israelites are marching for the first time since they received the law. What details of the march do you find?

4. Order in marching did not guarantee order in the camp. Read the complaints in Numbers 11:1-12. Identify three separate groups or individuals who complained.

5. From the following passages, give details of complaints.

   Numbers 11:1

   Numbers 11:4-6

Numbers 11:11-12

6. What was the immediate problem to be addressed in Numbers 11:13-15?

What deeper problem needed to be addressed?

How does Moses' response in this passage differ from his responses in last session's lesson?

Using as many adjectives and adverbs as possible, describe Moses' emotional, physical, and spiritual state.

Do you think the three were interrelated? Why/why not?

Can you think of a situation from your own life or from that of someone you know, in which pressures, responsibilities, and/or physical weariness prompted responses similar to Moses'?

7. What did God do about the problems, and in what order did He handle them? (Numbers 11:16-18)

What factors in this plan aided in easing the load Moses carried?

8. What specific complaint does God register against Israel? (Exodus 11:18-20)

How does God plan to punish Israel for this sin?

9. In what way does Numbers 11:21-24 demonstrate contrasting reactions on Moses' part?

In what way does it follow Moses' established pattern of obedience?

10. What example for your own life can you draw from this lesson?

Put Yourself in Moses' Sandals

11. You have been asked to give a talk on Reducing Spiritual Setbacks based on Numbers 11:10-30. Choose one of the following titles to work with or write one of your own. Jot down at least three statements you would use to make your point. Document them.

Mountaintop Experience Ends in Death Wish

Once Bold Leader Has Second Thoughts

Religious Leader Doubts Power of God

At least one point should explain how setbacks can happen, and one should give hope to listeners who may be fighting to avoid spiritual setbacks.

Growth Chart

12. *Growth Step: Guard against setbacks.* A permanent plateau is never reached in our spiritual growth. As you copy this session's Growth Step onto the Growth Chart on page 95, let it remind you to be on guard against those things which make you most susceptible to setbacks.

 DIGEST

Great moments of victory are often followed by devastating periods of depression. Our final lesson on wrestling with obedience focuses on the fact that permanent spiritual plateaus are never reached. We must constantly guard against those things which tempt us to disobey or make us vulnerable to setbacks.

Periods of discouragement are often triggered by the sheer weight of personal responsibility. The load becomes unbearable.

For example, a common responsibility of both mothers and managers is to listen to complaints. Whichever hat you wear, you know that this can be an energy-sapping chore. You may experience times when physical weariness combined with emotional conflicts drain you of the will to go on.

"Did I ask for this?"

"Get me out of here!"

"Must I be responsible for everything around here?"

Do these questions sound familiar? Certainly most women ask such questions at one time or another. And Moses asked them—after his great mountaintop experience where he stood so firmly on the promises of God and refused to budge. What happened?

From your discovery questions, you have seen that Moses took care of a myriad of details after the golden calf incident. As God's chosen leader, he was responsible for the detailed preparation of the recently delivered slaves. God kept them in Sinai for over a year to complete that preparation.

When they left Sinai it was the very first time they had marched in the precise order prescribed by the law. Order in marching did not guarantee order in the camp. The meticulous preparations didn't change the hearts of the people—not the receiving of God's law, not the erection of their place of worship, not the detailed attention to the logistics of their journey, not the miraculous provision of God.

The journey lasted three days and when they made camp, the people began to complain. It was a well established routine by now. They were tired of the monotonous diet and they longed for the good old days in Egypt. With Egypt 15 months behind them, they were becoming increasingly selective in how they remembered the old days.

Perhaps the weariness of the journey heightened both their complaints and Moses' complaints. For whatever reason, the Israelites were sick of manna, and Moses was sick of the Israelites. He wanted to be rid of the responsibility. (While God had previously given him this option, He did not give it to him now, just because he was weary!)

Recognize the Value of Proper Rest
Because we recognize that our battle is a spiritual one, we sometimes fail to reckon with the physical factors which affect this battle. Yet, a depletion of energy can lead to discouragement and even despair.

As a teenager, I lived on a street which was part of the historic Geronimo Trail. At the time the idea fascinated me only because I was eager to identify with Southwestern culture—all so new and different from our former home in the Midwest. It was years later that I discovered how fatigue had figured in Geronimo's surrender. The proud warrior who had often outsmarted and outmaneuvered his would-be captors was overcome by fatigue. He lost his will to go on. Weary in spirit, he found it preferable to surrender.

It was while living on the Geronimo Trail that I first experienced real fatigue. Working after school was too much for a young teenager experiencing sudden growth spurts. Every night I fell into bed, bone weary and wishing that I would not wake up for two months—at which time my temporary job would be ended. But I kept going, never once confiding in my parents about these inner struggles.

One Sunday my dam of emotions broke. In the middle of the church service, I began to cry uncontrollably. My mother took me home, put me to bed in a sunlit room, and ordered me to sleep. Later, after I had had a long nap, she brought me my favorite food on a tray. That experience was the beginning of my learning about the effects of physical weariness. Even the manner in which my mother responded was a learning point. While it took many years to put into practice all that I was learning, from that time on I understood an important principle. Proper rest is essential for our spirit as well as for our body.

Rearrange the Load
In Moses' case, an immediate problem triggered his outpouring of emotions—the people were tired of the manna and wanted meat to eat.

But there was another problem that surfaced. Moses felt as if he could no longer handle the task by himself. He needed reliable help to carry the load.

We all know "there's help and then there's help." In other words, not all help is going to ease the load. Not all coworkers or employees perform in such a way that the job of the supervisor is made easier.

It is interesting to note that God asked Moses to do the choosing; to choose men of proven ability; to bring the men before the tabernacle; and to stand with them. He promised to equip the men spiritually to provide the help that Moses needed.

When your load becomes so heavy that it affects you mentally, emotionally, and/or physically, perhaps you need to look for some ways to rearrange the load. Is there some chore or responsibility that you can drop at this time? Even if you hope to take it up at a later period of your life, perhaps you need relief right now.

Has some ministry proved to be too much for you? If so, can you prayerfully select a qualified friend who might assist you? Is it reasonable to ask your spouse or your children for more assistance in certain areas? This is not always an option, but if it is, perhaps now is the time to consider how you can work together and rearrange some of the load.

Recreation Helps
In spite of the current craze for physical fitness, or perhaps because of it, we are often reluctant to label recreation as a valid need. Yet if some form of recreation will make us less vulnerable to Satan's attacks, we must make every effort to schedule that recreation on a regular basis.

It has been confirmed many times that people who struggle with chronic depression benefit greatly from some form of regular exercise. Swimming, jogging, hiking, aerobics—all are positive ways to keep that bent toward depression under control.

Relieving stress is a chronic need in today's society. If stress is an ongoing problem for you, are you taking steps to deal with it?

One young working mom, takes a short swim late at night after her child is put to bed. "It really relaxes me," she declares.

One couple sets aside two Friday evenings each month just for themselves. They hire a baby-sitter for a few hours and go for a walk, window shop, wander around a mall, or even have a cozy twosome picnic somewhere.

Our own personal favorite stress chaser is to drive to a point overlooking the ocean, and watch the sun go down. In between those occasions, we put things aside and play a game. And I have found that whatever else I am doing, a regular swim (at least five days a week) is a necessity.

Spiritual Weapons

It is essential that we recognize our greatest weapons against spiritual setbacks are spiritual weapons. Study the Word, memorize it, do it. Pray regularly and thoughtfully. Fellowship with other believers, including some who are more mature than you. Such believers provide an example and are a source of encouragement.

Certainly, Moses' most important weapon against setbacks was his ongoing dialogue with God. But it is important to see that in the passage covered this week, Moses suffered a temporary setback because of reasons that could not be labeled "spiritual." If we fail to see that our physical, mental, and emotional condition makes us more vulnerable to Satan's attacks, then the enemy has already won a battle. If on the other hand, we can recognize the relationship between overwork, stress, fatigue, and spiritual setbacks, we will be far better equipped to guard against future setbacks.

❧ *PERSONAL RESPONSE JOURNAL* ❧

Thought Starter: What contributes to spiritual setbacks in your walk—too little time in the Word? Too little time in prayer? Too little encouragement from other believers? Too little rest? Too few "stress breaks"? Can you write a prayer to God about this need and of your need for help in minimizing setbacks?

_____

_____

_____

_____

_____

_____

_____

_____

_____

_____

🐚 *DIVERSIFY* 🐚

The following leader's guide provides you with specific suggestions to facilitate group discussion. You will find it most helpful if you encourage people to do the study before the group meeting. The objectives of this study are: first, to acquaint people with what the Bible actually says; and second, to show how the Bible applies to the practical problems of modern life. Encourage discussion, but try to keep the discussion focused on the lesson, avoiding tangents. Remind group members that the more time they spend studying the lesson, the more interesting and informed the discussion will be.

As each session comes to a close, help group members discuss and draw conclusions that are practical and applicable to their individual problem. Also spend time sharing and praying for each other. This will increase the benefit each group member gains from this study.

General Guidelines for Facilitating
Good Group Discussion

☐ Encourage discussion by asking several group members to contribute answers to a question. "What do the rest of you think?" or "Is there anything else which could be added?" are two ways of doing this.

☐ Be open and warm toward all contributions. Never bluntly reject what anyone says, even if you think the answer is incorrect. Instead, ask what the others in the group think.

☐ As group leader, be sure not to talk too much yourself. Try to redirect questions which you are asked. A discussion should move back and forth between members. The leader is to act as a moderator. As members of a group get to know one another better, the discussion will move more freely.

☐ Don't be afraid of pauses or long silences. People need time to think about the questions. Never answer your own question—either rephrase it or move on to another area for discussion.

☐ Watch hesitant members for an indication by facial expression or bodily posture that they have something to say and then give them an encouraging nod or speak their names.

☐ Discourage too talkative members from monopolizing the discussion by specifically directing questions to others. If necessary, speak privately to the overly talkative one about the need for discussion, and enlist her help in encouraging all to participate.

General Guidelines for Group Leaders

Preparation

☐ Pray for the Holy Spirit's guidance as you study, that you will be equipped to teach the lesson and make it appealing and applicable.

☐ Read through the entire lesson and any Bible passages or verses that are mentioned. Answer all the questions.

☐ Become familiar enough with the lesson that, if time in the group is running out, you know which questions could most easily be left out.

☐ Gather all the items you will need for the study: name tags, extra pens, extra Bibles.

The Meeting

☐ Start and end on time.

☐ Have everyone wear a name tag until group members know one another's name.

☐ Have each group member introduce herself or ask regular attenders to introduce guests.

☐ For each meeting, plan an activity (or ask an icebreaker question) to help group members get to know one another better.

❧ LEADER'S GUIDE 1 ❧

Objective
To help group members identify the place of commitment in the development of obedience to the Lord.

Personal Preparation
 ☐ Before you begin, read the introductory section.
 ☐ Read Exodus 1–2 in one sitting.
 ☐ Complete the *Discovery Time* section for chapter 1.
 ☐ Read the *Digest*. Jot down personal illustrations which may help you better apply this lesson to your group.
 ☐ Pray for those who will be joining the group in this very first session. Pray that God will lead each individual to assess her spiritual needs in the area of choices/commitments which need to be made.

Group Time
 ☐ Emphasize that in this lesson, both Moses and his parents were confronted with hard choices. State that just as they made the right choices, so must we today.
 ☐ Remind the group that there is a 400-year gap between Genesis 50 and Exodus 1. State: **Our first two questions will bring us up to date as to what has happened to the descendants of Jacob in the intervening years.**
 ☐ Ask a volunteer to share her findings for question 1. Then proceed around the room through Question 3.
 ☐ Question 4 is the first of several to call for interpretative answers based on the Scripture indicated. Whenever possible, allow time for several to respond to this type of question. Begin with the next person (proceeding around the room) in order. After she has shared her findings, ask: **Did anyone come up with something essentially different which you would like to add?**
 ☐ Since the more creative ones may be anxious to read their "tabloid reporting" call for a volunteer to answer Question 5. Allow several volunteers to read answers if time permits.
 ☐ Questions 6–8 call for personal conclusions based on the Scripture indicated. Follow the procedure outlined for Question 4.
 ☐ Question 10. If the class fails to make the connection, point out that in Exodus 2:22, Moses is calling himself a stranger in a strange land when he names his son. This seems to point to the fact that from the time he gave up his standing as the son of Pharaoh's daughter, his heart was always with the slaves in Egypt.

☐ When you come to Question 15, point out that it is a personal question and not to be shared with the group. Encourage each one to think about it carefully and answer it if she has not already done so.

☐ Help the women find the Growth Chart on page 95. Explain the significance of the reverse numbering. (Growth charts always begin at the bottom and work up.) Encourage them to fill in the chart each week and to be creative in illustrating it as well.

☐ Encourage them to make use of the Personal Response Journal and emphasize that it is not to be shared with the group.

☐ Encourage the group to share prayer requests. Close with a time of prayer for one another. Include the following request: **Help us begin today to make the right choices for the development of obedience in our lives.**

🍂 *LEADER'S GUIDE 2* 🍂

Objective
To encourage group members to face openly and honestly all obstacles (including doubts) which hinder obedience.

Personal Preparation
□ Thoroughly familiarize yourself with this passage.
□ Complete the *Discovery Time* section.
□ Read the *Digest* section.
□ Pray for sensitivity toward the group with regard to emphasis. Some women may struggle more with feelings of inadequacy. Others may have deeply hidden doubts about their faith.

Group Time
□ Emphasize that in this passage Moses is being forced to remember his past failure. God is asking him to do something which he has already tried to do and failed. Point out that he has lived with this failure for 40 years.
□ Question 1. Proceed around the room allowing each person to answer or contribute.
□ Question 2. Moses traded in prince's robes for shepherd's garb. Life in the palace included the company of many people, conversations, intellectual stimulation. As a shepherd, he was alone much of the time with only the sheep for company.
□ Questions 3–5. Have the passage read aloud as questions are answered.
□ Question 6. Exodus 4:1, 5 is the key to the correct answer here. Help the group see that God gave the signs so that Israel would believe the Lord had appeared to Moses.
□ Question 7. Help the group see that Moses is recalling how his Hebrew brethren accused him, "Who made you a prince and a judge over us?" (Exodus 2:14) He seeks assurance that if he returns to Egypt, Israel will know that God has sent him.
□ Questions 8–10. These questions should lead to some personal application.
□ Questions 11–12. Point out the concluding illustration from the *Digest*—the four-point sermon on "What to do with your doubts."
□ Question 13. State: **I hope you have all answered question 13. If you feel it's too personal, you need not share your answer.**
□ *Growth Step* Ask your group members if they have filled out their Growth Charts.

♣ LEADER'S GUIDE 3 ♣

Objective
To encourage group members to obey God whether they want to or not.

Personal Preparation
□ As you prepare this week's lesson, keep in mind the many objections Moses has raised—especially his last one (Exodus 4:13). Think about the various examples of people who were reluctant to obey God. Try to discern how these examples differ from one another. Think about the example Moses set for believers today as he obeyed God in spite of all his questions, protests, and reluctance.

□ Highlight the *Digest* section which refers to Jonah's determined disobedience. Be prepared to review this material with question 10.

□ Do some illustrations on your Growth Chart. For example, on Step #1 you could draw a tent, depicting Midian; for Step #2, a series of question marks; for Step #3, a motto such as "Just Say Yes."

Group Time
□ Question 1. Begin questions by calling on one person and proceeding around the circle for succeeding questions.

□ Question 2. Help group members see that Moses is a model because he obeyed even when he clearly did not want to.

□ Question 3. These passages present an interesting contrast. Moses had many questions. The Israelites demonstrated "instant belief." For the second half of the question, the group should readily see that Israel, in fact, became very disobedient while Moses learned to obey by obeying.

□ Question 5. The most accurate answer should reflect information given in Exodus 4:5.

□ Questions 6–7. After these questions are answered, emphasize that in spite of their fears, Israel did obey God.

□ Questions 8–9. Help the group discover that God counts obedience as faith.

□ Question 10. Note that Gideon repeatedly asked for a sign that it was really God who was sending him (Judges 6:17ff). While there are many similarities between Gideon's reluctant obedience and Moses', Jonah is a different case. Help the group see that Jonah deliberately disobeyed from the beginning.

□ Question 15. This is a thought question to be pondered privately.

□ *Growth Chart* Encourage group members to doodle, draw stick figures, or use stickers to illustrate. Share ideas from your own illustrated chart.

❧ LEADER'S GUIDE 4 ❧

Objective
To encourage continued obedience amid discouraging circumstances.

Personal Preparation
☐ Read this week's passage aloud as you begin your preparation.
☐ Complete the *Discovery Time* section.
☐ Read the *Digest* with highlighter in hand. Make notes of any additional illustrations you may use to show (1) how circumstances discourage believers or (2) how believers persist in obedience in spite of discouraging circumstances.
☐ Plan to include a review of the *Digest* in this week's session.
☐ Pray for your group individually.

Group Time
☐ Questions 1–5. Proceed around the group with the initial questions, drawing out the exact details of the scenario recorded in Exodus 5:5-21. Emphasize the various problems which arose as a result of Moses' and Aaron's audience with Pharaoh. If the group has difficulty with question 5, remind them that when a plan goes sour, the leader is usually the first to be blamed.
☐ Question 6. After both sections are answered, emphasize to the group that although Moses is very discouraged, he is doing the right thing. He is spreading his discouragement before the Lord.
☐ Questions 7–8. Allow several to share answers for these two questions.
☐ Question 9. In the *King James Version*, the pronoun *I* occurs 18 times in 8 verses. Obviously, God wants to reassure Moses that He is in control.
☐ Question 10. Allow one person to answer the five parts of this question. Then ask: **Does anyone have something essentially different to add?**
☐ Question 12. Emphasize the importance of Moses' continued obedience despite his disillusionment.
☐ Question 13. After one member has shared her answers to this question, allow several others to give additional input.

❧LEADER'S GUIDE 5❧

Objective
To help group members surrender self-imposed responsibility for success in ministry.

Personal Preparation
☐ Scan the suggested passage, familiarizing yourself with the highlights.
☐ Complete the *Discovery Time* section.
☐ Read the *Digest*, making notes of the points which stand out to you.
☐ On a note card, make a list of points you have gleaned from *Discovery Time* and *Digest* sections that will help you meet this session's objective. At what points of the group time can you logically interject these points?

Group Time
☐ Questions 1–2. Allow two group members to share their answers. The purpose of these questions is to focus on the exact nature of Moses' responsibility.
☐ Question 4. Ask someone to read Exodus 8:8 aloud. This is the first time Pharaoh suggests he will allow Israel to go.
☐ Question 5. If necessary have Exodus 8:15 read aloud to discover the result of the judgment of frogs.
☐ Question 6. For differences and effect, note Exodus 8:18-19.
☐ Question 7. Read 8:22 carefully for the answer to this question.
☐ Question 8. After a group member has shared her answer, restate the warning from 8:29. If no one has suggested the possibility, ask: **Do you think Moses might have been hoping to nudge Pharaoh into action at this point?**
☐ Question 9. Show that Pharaoh called for proof that God had done as He said He would, but that the proof had no effect on him (Exodus 9:7).
☐ Question 10. Allow time to establish the information called for in this question. Conclude by saying: **If God had only been concerned with delivering Israel, He could have done it without the plagues. But He had a purpose in the plagues and Moses didn't always understand that purpose.**
☐ Question 11. Allow room for different opinions but try to draw out that Moses had become more focused on obedience and less on results (or lack of results).

⋐ *LEADER'S GUIDE 6* ⋑

Objective
To inspire group members to persist in their study of God's Word—
especially His promises to believers.

Personal Preparation
☐ Read the assigned passage in one sitting.
☐ Complete the *Discovery Time* section. Pay careful attention to questions 5–9.
☐ Read *Digest,* highlighting headings and subheadings as you go as well as those parts which will illuminate questions 5–9.
☐ If your group includes women who are currently facing circumstances which make trusting God's promises difficult, spend some time in prayer especially for them.

Group Time
☐ Question 1. Ask that the references be read before the first participant shares her answer.
☐ Question 2. Exodus 11:1 establishes the fact that this is the last plague. Allow one person to give her findings. Call for additional input until you are satisfied all details are established.
☐ Questions 5–9 are crucial to an understanding of Moses' growth. Take time to establish all the details as the group shares its findings.
☐ Question 5. Draw out that the Passover was a celebration of the Israelites' deliverance from Egypt.
☐ Question 6. Emphasize that in the first Passover they were celebrating deliverance, but they were still slaves in Egypt.
☐ Question 7. Note that while all Israel observed this celebration, Moses was the instigator. In obedience to God's command, he led the celebration of deliverance.
☐ Questions 8–9. Allow ample time for participants to share their thoughts on these two questions.
☐ Question 11. Allow several to share their findings for this question. Emphasize that Israel teaches us how important obedience is to faith. Refer to the heading, "Israel's Faith" in the *Digest.*

❧ LEADER'S GUIDE 7 ❧

Objective
To help the group develop a better understanding of how to stand on God's promises.

Personal Preparation
☐ Read the assigned passage.
☐ Complete the *Discovery Time* section.
☐ Read *Digest*, highlighting sections you may wish to emphasize in group time.
☐ Pray for your group as they study this session's lesson, that they will be open to the Holy Spirit's teaching.

Group Time
☐ Question 1. Ask that the first participant read the indicated passage and share her findings. If necessary, call for additional input until the details are established.
☐ Question 2. Again, ask for the indicated passage to be read before the participant shares her answer. Refer to Exodus 4:15-16 to discover the extent and the basis of Aaron's potential.
☐ Question 4. If the class finds this question difficult, do an in-class exercise. Ask half to turn to Exodus 6:1-8 and half to Exodus 32:11-14. Together, isolate all the promises in the first passage. Then look for possible references to those promises in the second passage.
☐ Question 5. Allow time for several to share their findings. Ask: **What additional insight on this question did you gain from the Digest?**
☐ Question 7. Be prepared for some questions from the group regarding God's severe judgment. Remind them that in God's plan to move the nation from Egypt to Canaan, it was necessary to judge the disobedient in order to preserve the nation. As God's chosen leader Moses acted as judge and then wept over the people's sin.
☐ Questions 8–10. After the participants have answered these questions, take time to emphasize that Moses finds himself stripped of all resources other than the promises of God.
☐ Question 13. Allow each participant to share her answer to this question.

❧ *LEADER'S GUIDE 8* ❧

Objective
To help the group recognize and reduce those factors which make them vulnerable to spiritual setbacks.

Personal Preparation
□ Read the assigned passage carefully, giving attention to the many details.

□ Do the *Discovery Time* section. Take ample time for Question 11. Be prepared to share your example with the group.

□ Read *Digest*, highlighting main headings and any portions you may wish to emphasize.

□ Pray for your group members that each will achieve the growth steps necessary for a more complete obedience.

Group Time
□ Question 1. After the first participant shares her findings, ask: **In terms of stress, what does it mean to be responsible for so many details in so many different areas?**

□ Questions 3–4. After these two questions are answered, allow some time for discussion before proceeding. Ask: **Do you think people tend to complain more when they are tired?**

□ Question 6. The immediate problem was Israel's hunger for meat. The deeper problem was Moses' weariness and discouragement. If the group fails to make this point, have the passage read aloud and talk it through.

□ Question 7. Refer to the *Digest* section under "Rearranging the Load" to emphasize how God handled the problem. Encourage group members to share personal problems or solutions on handling stress.

□ Question 9. Help the group to see that once again Moses does as God commands, despite his questions and doubts about the plan.

□ Question 11. If time permits, allow all participants to share their speech material. To conclude discussion, point out that each of the three headlines suggest what can happen to the most faithful, mature believer who is overstressed. Review the *Digest* main headings as practical ways to combat stress.

□ *Growth Chart* Ask the group members to turn in their books to the Chart. Review the steps. Close in prayer, asking that each person achieve the growth that God desires for her.